What's in this book

This book belongs to

_____

1 Learn about China 中国知多少

Country profile 国家概况

China is a country in Asia. Here are some facts about China.

Country: China, 中国 (Zhongguo)
China is officially called the People's Republic of China (PRC).

Capital: Beijing
Located in northern China, Beijing is the political and cultural centre of China.

the Li River

Size: Around 9,600,000 km^2
China looks like a huge rooster on the map. There are many rivers, lakes, mountains and forests in China.

the Himalayas

the Yellow River

Population: Over 1.3 billion
China has the largest population in the world.

Ethnic groups: 56
Besides the largest ethnic group, Han, which makes up over 90% of the population, there are also 55 ethnic minorities.

Language: There is only one writing system in China, but people speak different dialects.

Written	Spoken	
Official	Official	Main dialects
Standardized Chinese characters	Putonghua (Standardized form of the spoken Chinese based on Mandarin)	Mandarin, Wu, Xiang, Gan, Hakka, Min, Cantonese

Symbols of China 中国象征

Is there anything that reminds you of China? Look at some symbols of China.

The Chinese dragon: It is regarded as a divine creature and a symbol of good luck and power. Chinese people call themselves Descendants of the Dragon.

The giant panda: It is China's national treasure and the symbol of WWF. It is listed as one of the vulnerable species in the world.

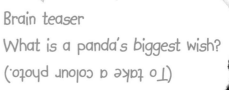

Brain teaser
What is a panda's biggest wish?
(To take a colour photo.)

The Great Wall: In ancient times, it was built for protection against invasions. Today, it is a World Heritage site.

Chinese kungfu: It is not only about fighting and self-defense, it can also strengthen the body and mind.

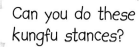

Can you do these kungfu stances?

2 Chinese zodiac 生肖

1 Do you know the 12 zodiac animals? Learn about them.

hóu
猴

niú
牛

hǔ
虎

mǎ
马

lóng
龙

The Chinese zodiac is a cycle of 12 lunar years. Each year is represented by an animal. The animals appear in a fixed order.

zhū
猪

jī
鸡

shǔ
鼠

tù
兔

yáng
羊

shé
蛇

gǒu
狗

2 The 12 zodiac animals appear in the following order. Look at the pictures on page 6 again and number them.

1 rat   2 ox   3 tiger   4 rabbit

5 dragon   6 snake   7 horse   8 sheep

9 monkey   10 rooster   11 dog   12 pig

3 Which zodiac animal sign were you born under? Look at the information below to find out.

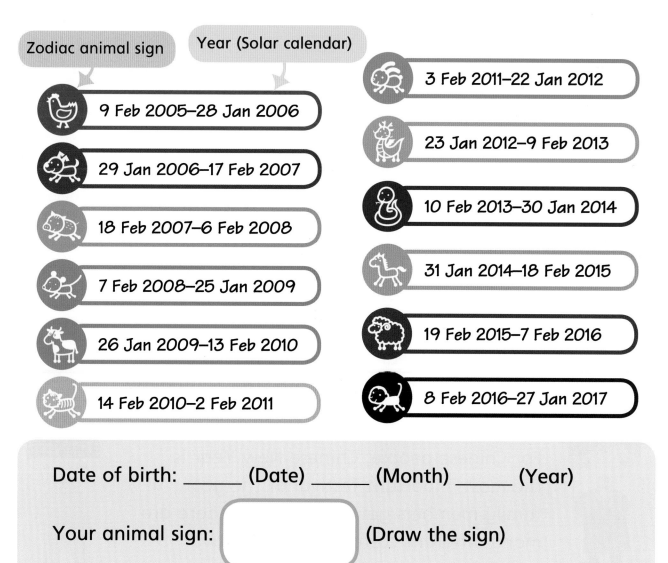

Zodiac animal sign

Year (Solar calendar)

9 Feb 2005–28 Jan 2006

29 Jan 2006–17 Feb 2007

18 Feb 2007–6 Feb 2008

7 Feb 2008–25 Jan 2009

26 Jan 2009–13 Feb 2010

14 Feb 2010–2 Feb 2011

3 Feb 2011–22 Jan 2012

23 Jan 2012–9 Feb 2013

10 Feb 2013–30 Jan 2014

31 Jan 2014–18 Feb 2015

19 Feb 2015–7 Feb 2016

8 Feb 2016–27 Jan 2017

Date of birth: _____ (Date) _____ (Month) _____ (Year)

Your animal sign: [   ] (Draw the sign)

3 Festivals 节日

Traditional Chinese festivals 传统中国节日

Traditional Chinese festivals are celebrated according to the Chinese Lunar Calendar. Learn the names of the most popular ones.

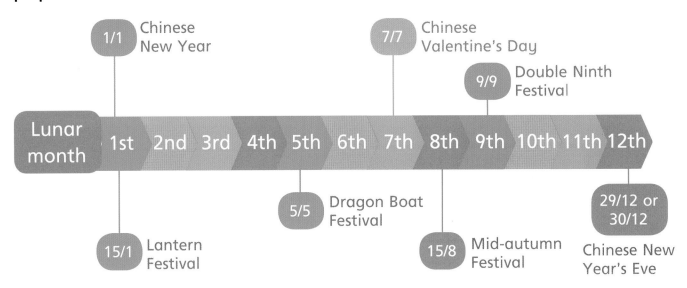

| 1/1 Chinese New Year | 7/7 Chinese Valentine's Day |
| 9/9 Double Ninth Festival |

| Lunar month | 1st | 2nd | 3rd | 4th | 5th | 6th | 7th | 8th | 9th | 10th | 11th | 12th |

| 15/1 Lantern Festival | 5/5 Dragon Boat Festival | 15/8 Mid-autumn Festival | 29/12 or 30/12 Chinese New Year's Eve |

Chinese New Year (Spring Festival)

1 Learn about Chinese New Year.

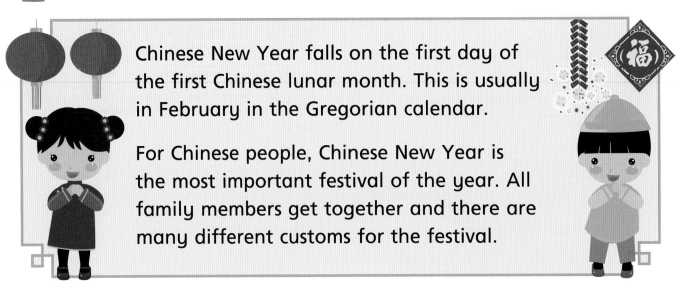

Chinese New Year falls on the first day of the first Chinese lunar month. This is usually in February in the Gregorian calendar.

For Chinese people, Chinese New Year is the most important festival of the year. All family members get together and there are many different customs for the festival.

Decorations, red packets and traditional snacks represent good luck, good health and good fortune. People use unique sayings to greet each other and express good wishes.

New Year decorations

Red packets and traditional snacks

Greetings

There are various celebrations. Some people go to the temples to make wishes.

Dragon dance

Parade

Temple fair

Today, Chinese New Year is celebrated in many major cities around the world.

Beijing, China

San Francisco, USA

London, UK

2 Learn to make Chinese New Year decorations. Colour the words black or gold.

新　年　快　乐

Dragon Boat Festival

1 Learn about the Dragon Boat Festival.

The Dragon Boat Festival falls on the fifth day of the fifth lunar month. This is usually in June in the Gregorian calendar.

During this festival, people race dragon boats and eat *zongzi*. People believe that this festival commemorates the famous poet Qu Yuan.

Dragon boats are shaped like dragons. Accompanied by rapid drum beats, the oarers pull the oars.

Zongzi are glutinous rice dumplings wrapped in reed or bamboo leaves.

2 Look at the posters of the Dragon Boat Festival. Design your own and show it to your friends.

Mid-Autumn Festival

1 Learn about the Mid-Autumn Festival.

The Mid-Autumn Festival falls on the fifteenth day of the eighth lunar month. This is usually in October for the Gregorian calendar.

This festival is celebrated at night under the autumn full moon. A popular legend goes that Chang'e, the Moon Goddess, lives on the moon.

At the Mid-Autumn Festival, family and friends get together to watch the full moon and eat mooncakes to show family unity. Children like to play with lanterns.

2 Look at the traditional lanterns and design one for yourself. Show it to your friends.

4 Food and drink 饮食

Chinese cuisine 中国菜

1 Chinese cuisine is an important part of Chinese culture. Learn about it.

Chinese cuisine emphasizes colour, flavour and taste.

This means, shape and nutrition of a dish are also important.

2 Chinese cuisines vary in styles. The 'Eight Cuisines' of China are from these provinces.

Eight Cuisines of China

1 Anhui cuisine
2 Guangdong cuisine
3 Hunan cuisine
4 Sichuan cuisine
5 Zhejiang cuisine
6 Shandong cuisine
7 Jiangsu cuisine
8 Fujian cuisine

3 Look at the dishes and learn their names. Discuss with your friend which dishes the children are describing.

Stinky tofu, Anhui

Oyster omelette, Fujian

Roast goose, Guangdong

Steamed fish head with chilli, Hunan

Yangzhou fried rice, Jiangsu

Kung Pao chicken, Sichuan

Longjing shrimps, Zhejiang

Braised sea cucumber, Shandong

I love spicy food! Which dishes are spicy?

It smells funny but tastes good!

Wow! Crispy skin and juicy meat!

Seafood is my favourite.

I'm a rice lover!

4 Did you know that the staple foods in southern China and northern China are different?

Rice is a major staple food in southern China. Cooked rice, usually white rice, is the most commonly eaten type.

We eat rice every day.

Flour-based foods, such as noodles, Chinese dumplings and steamed buns, are the most popular staple foods in northern China.

5 Desserts are also popular in Chinese cuisine. They are served after meals. Look at a few examples.

Cold or hot	Cold	Hot

6 Tea plays an important role in Chinese dining culture. Have you tried Chinese tea before?

Tips on Chinese dining 中餐小知识

Look at some tips on Chinese dining.

In traditional Chinese dining, dishes are shared between everyone. In restaurants, round tables with a turntable at the centre are often used for easy sharing. Tea is almost always provided.

Chopsticks are the main eating utensils in Chinese dining. They can be used to cut and pick up food.

Practise using chopsticks with me!

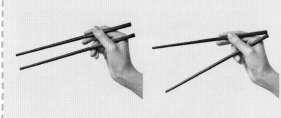  

5 Tourist destinations 旅游目的地

Reasons for visiting China 来中国旅游的原因

Each year, tourists from around the world visit China. Do you know what they love about China? Look at the pictures and see what China has to offer.

Natural scenery

Architecture

Culture

History

Life style

Popular tourist destinations 热门旅游目的地

1 These ten places are among the most popular tourist destinations in China. Have you heard of them before?

Beijing Chengdu Guangzhou Hangzhou Hong Kong

Lijiang Macau Shanghai Xi'an Yangshuo

2 Beijing, the capital city of China, is a place where old meets new. Look at some of the historic sites and modern tourist attractions. Which one do you like best?

the Forbidden City

the Summer Palace

Beijing

Sanlitun

the National Theatre

the Great Wall

3 Look at the popular tourist attractions in the other nine places. Help the children find the most suitable places to visit.

Wolong National Nature Reserve, Chengdu

the Terracotta Army, Xi'an

Old Town of Lijiang, Lijiang

the Li River, Yangshuo

Canton Tower, Guangzhou

Lujiazui skyline, Shanghai

West Lake, Hangzhou

the Avenue of Stars,
Hong Kong

the Ruins of St Paul's, Macao

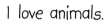

I love animals.

I like taking pictures of
beautiful sceneries.

I'm interested in
Chinese history.

6 Arts 艺术

China's 5,000 years of history has given rise to its unique and various art forms. The following pictures show some of them. Look carefully. Complete the tasks and show your work to your friends.

Painting, calligraphy and literature

Painting

Literature

Calligraphy

Complete the Chinese painting.

Handicraft, sculpture and carving

Handicraft

Sculpture and carving

Paint a Chinese vase.

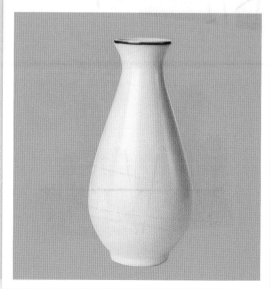

Performing art

Paint an opera mask.

Architecture

Draw a Chinese-style building.

OXFORD
UNIVERSITY PRESS

Oxford University Press is a department of the University of Oxford.
It furthers the University's objective of excellence in research, scholarship,
and education by publishing worldwide. Oxford is a registered trade mark of
Oxford University Press in the UK and in certain other countries

Published in Hong Kong by
Oxford University Press (China) Limited
39th Floor, One Kowloon, 1 Wang Yuen Street, Kowloon Bay,
Hong Kong

First Edition published in 2017

China National Publications Import & Export (Group) Corporation is an authorized distributor of
Oxford Elementary Chinese.

Please contact content@cnpiec.com.cn or 86-10-65856782

ISBN: 978-0-19-082365-8

10 9 8 7 6 5 4 3